THE
TOTALLY
COOKIES
COOKBOOK

Printed in Singapore.
The Totally Cookies Cookbook is produced by becker&mayer!, Ltd.
Cover illustration and design: Dick Witt
Interior illustration: Carolyn Vibbert
Interior design and typesetting: Susan Hernday

Library of Congress Cataloging-in-Publication Data
Siegel, Helene.
    The Totally Cookies Cookbook / by Helene Siegel and Karen Gillingham.
        p.   cm.
    ISBN: 0-89087-757-2
    1. Cookies.   I. Gillingham, Karen.   II. Title.
TX772.S45   1995
641.8′654—dc20

Celestial Arts Publishing
P.O. Box 7123
Berkeley, CA 94707

Other cookbooks in this series:
The Totally Chile Pepper Cookbook
The Totally Garlic Cookbook
The Totally Mushroom Cookbook
The Totally Corn Cookbook
The Totally Muffins Cookbook
The Totally Coffee Cookbook
The Totally Teatime Cookbook

THE
TOTALLY
COOKIES
COOKBOOK

by
Helene Siegel
and
Karen Gillingham

Illustrations by Carolyn Vibbert

CELESTIAL ARTS
BERKELEY, CA

CONVERSIONS

LIQUID

1 Tbsp = 15 ml
½ cup = 2 fl. oz = 60 ml
1 cup = 8 fl. oz = 250 ml

DRY

¼ cup = 4 Tbsp = 2 oz = 60 g
1 cup = ½ pound = 8 oz = 250 g

FLOUR

½ cup = 60 g
1 cup = 4 oz = 125 g

TEMPERATURE

400° F = 200°C = gas mark 6
375° F = 190°C = gas mark 5
350°F = 175°C = gas mark 4

MISCELLANEOUS

2 Tbsp butter = 1 oz = 30 g
1 inch = 2.5 cm
all-purpose flour = plain flour
baking soda = bicarbonate of soda
brown sugar = demerara sugar
confectioners' sugar = icing sugar
heavy cream = double cream
molasses = black treacle
raisins = sultanas
rolled oats = oat flakes
semisweet chocolate = plain chocolate
sugar = caster sugar

CONTENTS

Ever since we attempted, in a strange nutritional experiment back in the 1950s, to eat nothing but chocolate cookies and an occasional glass of milk, cookies have been a favorite food. We can say no to cake and snub a tub of ice cream, but slip a plate of cookies under our collective noses and you might as well just kiss those size-eight pants goodbye.

How could it be otherwise?

In these days of crass calorie counting and hurried lives, cookies are more appropriate than ever. They are small enough to be eaten guiltlessly at elegant dinner parties or casual teas. They can be made in advance, eaten standing up, or at least without silverware, stuffed in a pocket or purse for quick getaways and taken with coffee, tea, sweet wines and, of course, milk. They travel well, make consistently excellent gifts, and as

bribes for toddlers, they are without compare.

This collection of personal
favorites includes icons like chocolate
chip and peanut butter cookies with slight
twists; classic lemon bars and brownies as well
as rich, chewy apricot bars and miniature linzer
tarts; ethnic favorites like crunchy biscotti,
melt-in-your-mouth madeleines and tender
rugelach; wheat bran and sesame seed biscuits
for health–addled adults; and kids' cookies for the
hopelessly immature.

We've included something for everyone, we
hope, because everyone deserves a great cookie.
Some are even willing to steal for it.

Who stole the cookie from the cookie jar?
Who stole the cookie from the cookie jar?
Who me? Yes you. Couldn't be. Then who?
Who stole the cookie from the cookie jar?

ICONS

CHOCOLATE CHIP COOKIES

For cookie purists, the standard recipe for classic Toll House cookies. A tough act to follow.

2 sticks butter, softened
3/4 cup sugar
3/4 cup brown sugar
2 eggs
2 teaspoons vanilla
2 1/4 cups all-purpose flour
1 teaspoon baking powder
1 teaspoon salt
1 (12-ounce) package semisweet
    chocolate chips
3/4 cup toasted chopped walnuts,
    optional

Preheat oven to 350 degrees F.
Grease cookie sheet.

Cream butter until light and fluffy. Slowly add sugars, continuing to cream until smooth and light. Beat in eggs, one at a time, and then beat in vanilla.

In another bowl, stir together flour, baking powder, and salt. Add to creamed mixture and slowly beat until flour just disappears. Stir in chips and nuts, if desired.

Drop by generous tablespoonfuls, about 2 inches apart, on prepared sheets and bake 10 to 15 minutes, just until edges are golden. Cool on sheet 1 minute, then transfer to racks to cool.

The dough can be chilled for about ½ hour and then shaped into a log, wrapped in plastic, and stored in refrigerator. Just cut into ½-inch slices and bake as above.

MAKES ABOUT 40

WHITE CHOCOLATE PECAN CHIPS

Here is a caramely variation on the chip-and-nut theme.

1 stick butter, softened
3/4 cup brown sugar
1 egg
1 teaspoon vanilla
1 1/4 cups all-purpose flour
1/2 teaspoon baking soda
1/4 teaspoon salt
1/4 teaspoon cinnamon
1/2 cup roughly chopped
   white chocolate or vanilla chips
3/4 cup pecan halves, toasted and
   roughly chopped

Preheat oven to 350 degrees F. Lightly grease cookie sheets.

Beat together butter and sugar until smooth and creamy. Beat in egg and vanilla.

In another bowl, combine flour, baking soda, salt, and cinnamon. Add to butter mixture and stir just to combine. Stir in white chocolate and pecans.

Drop by generous tablespoonfuls on prepared sheet and bake 18 to 20 minutes, until edges brown and tops set. Transfer to racks to cool.

MAKES 26

PEANUT BUTTER CHIPPERS

You don't have to love peanut butter to fall in love with these crumbly, crunchy morsels dotted with milk chocolate chips. They bear a striking resemblance to peanut butter cups.

2 sticks butter, softened
$^3/_4$ cup sugar
$^3/_4$ cup brown sugar
1$^1/_2$ cups chunky peanut butter
2 eggs
1 teaspoon vanilla
2$^3/_4$ cups all-purpose flour
1 teaspoon baking soda
1 teaspoon salt
1 cup milk chocolate chips

Preheat oven to 350 degrees F. Grease cookie sheets.

In large mixing bowl, cream butter until soft and light. Beat in sugars to blend. Beat in peanut butter, eggs, one at a time, and vanilla.

In another bowl, combine flour, baking soda, and salt. Add to creamed mixture and slowly beat just until flour disappears. Stir in chips.

Drop by tablespoonfuls on prepared sheet, leaving 2 inches between each. Lightly flatten twice with prongs of fork to make criss-cross pattern. Bake 15 to 18 minutes, until edges are just golden and centers barely set. Transfer to racks to cool.

MAKES ABOUT 46

OATMEAL RAISIN COOKIES

Coconut is the secret ingredient that gives these chewy tidbits distinction.

1 stick butter, softened
1 cup brown sugar
1 egg
1 1/2 cups rolled oats
1 cup all-purpose flour
1/2 cup unsweetened grated coconut
1/2 teaspoon baking soda
1 teaspoon cinnamon
1/4 teaspoon salt
1 cup raisins

Preheat oven to 400 degrees F. Grease cookie sheets.

In large mixing bowl, cream butter and sugar until light. Beat in egg.

In another bowl, combine oats, flour, coconut, baking soda, cinnamon, and salt. Add to creamed mixture and beat well. Stir in raisins.

Drop by generous tablespoonfuls, 2 inches apart, on greased sheet. Bake 10 to 12 minutes, just until set. Transfer to racks to cool.

MAKES 25

Keeping Cookies

Cookies are best stored in cookie jars or tins, but be finicky about what you store together. Do not mix crisp and chewy types or they are likely to change character dramatically.

All but the crispiest cookies may be frozen for future munching. Just wrap in aluminum foil or in ziplock freezer bags. Remove from packing and defrost at room temperature. It only takes about 15 minutes to defrost most cookies.

ALMOND RASPBERRY THUMBPRINTS

We like the flecks of brown the almond skins give these cozy jelly cookies. Purchase whole or sliced almonds and then grind in the food processor. Extra ground nuts can always be frozen.

1 ¼ cups finely ground almonds, with skins
1 ½ cups all-purpose flour
½ teaspoon baking soda
½ teaspoon salt
1 stick butter, softened
½ cup brown sugar
2 eggs, separated
2 teaspoons Amaretto or ½ teaspoon almond extract
¼ cup raspberry jam

Preheat oven to 350 F. Lightly grease cookie sheets. Place ¾ cup ground almonds in small bowl and set aside.

Toss together flour, ½ cup ground almonds, baking soda, and salt.

In another large mixing bowl, cream butter until light and smooth. Add sugar and beat until fluffy. Beat in egg yolks and Amaretto or extract. Add flour mixture and slowly beat until flour disappears and dough holds together when pressed.

Whisk egg whites in small bowl until foamy. Break off tablespoon-sized pieces of dough and roll between palms to form ball. Dip in egg whites to coat and then roll in reserved almonds. Place on cookie sheet and press crater in center with the back of ½ teaspoon measure or thumb tip. Repeat until sheet is full.

Bake about 15 minutes, until nuts on the edges just begin to color. While still hot, immediately repress hole in center with back of measuring spoon. Transfer to racks to cool and fill each with ½ teaspoon raspberry jam.

MAKES ABOUT 20

SUGAR COOKIES

For cookie purists—crumbly, sugary, vanilla-packed sugar wafers with a nice ragged edge. For more experienced bakers, this is a good dough for rolling and cutting.

> 2 sticks butter, softened
> ³/₄ cup sugar
> ¹/₂ teaspoon salt
> 1 egg yolk
> 1¹/₂ teaspoons vanilla
> ¹/₂ cup chopped pecans
> 2 cups all-purpose flour
> sugar

Preheat oven to 350 degrees F. Lightly grease cookie sheets or line with parchment.

Cream butter and sugar until light and fluffy. Beat in salt, egg yolk, and vanilla.

Beat in pecans. Then add flour and stir just until it disappears and dough holds together when pressed.

Roll generous tablespoonfuls of dough between palms to make balls. Place each on cookie sheet, allowing plenty of space for spreading. Then generously coat the bottom of a small glass with butter, dip into a bowl of sugar to coat and press each ball to flatten. The edges should look cracked.

Bake 13 to 15 minutes, until edges turn golden brown. Transfer to racks to cool.

MAKES 36

PECAN SHORTBREAD

Shortbreads are easy to make and universally loved. These have a hint of butterscotch from brown sugar and cinnamon.

2 sticks butter, softened
1/3 cup confectioners' sugar
1/3 cup brown sugar
2 teaspoons rum or vanilla
1 cup all-purpose flour
1 1/4 cups cake flour
1/2 teaspoon salt
1/4 teaspoon cinnamon
24 pecan halves

Preheat oven to 350 degress F.

In large bowl of electric mixer, cream butter until smooth and fluffy. Add sugars and cream to blend. Beat in rum or vanilla.

In another bowl, combine flours, salt, and cinnamon. Add to creamed mixture and mix until combined. Turn out onto floured board, press into circle and lightly roll with floured pin to ½-inch thick circle.

Cut out with round cookie cutter or small glass dipped in flour. Transfer cookies to ungreased baking sheet, press a pecan half in the center of each and bake just until set, 18 to 20 minutes. Transfer to racks to cool. Re-roll remaining dough scraps, handling as briefly as possible, and repeat until no dough remains.

MAKES 24

HERMITS

These classic New England cookies have extraordinary keeping qualities. They were said to accompany sailors on long ocean voyages.

1¾ cups all-purpose flour
¾ teaspoon cinnamon
½ teaspoon ground nutmeg
¼ teaspoon ground cloves
½ teaspoon baking soda
½ teaspoon salt
1 stick butter, softened
1 cup brown sugar
1 egg
¾ cup buttermilk
1 cup raisins, coarsely chopped
¾ cup chopped walnuts

Preheat oven to 375 degrees F.

Sift together flour, cinnamon, nutmeg, cloves, soda and salt. Set aside.

In large bowl, beat butter until light. Gradually beat in brown sugar, then egg and buttermilk. Add dry ingredients and beat until smooth. Stir in raisins and walnuts.

Drop by rounded tablespoonfuls onto ungreased baking sheet. Bake about 15 minutes or until edges are golden.

Let cool 1 minute on baking sheets, then transfer to rack to cool.

MAKES ABOUT 24

SNICKERDOODLES

Snickerdoodles are an unfussy sugar cookie with a crackled top, an extra dollop of cinnamon sugar and a terrific name.

1¾ cups all-purpose flour
½ teaspoon ground nutmeg
¾ teaspoon baking powder
½ teaspoon salt
1 stick butter, room temperature
¾ cup plus 2 tablespoons sugar
1 egg
1 teaspoon vanilla
1 tablespoon cinnamon

Preheat oven to 350 degrees F. Grease baking sheets.

Combine flour, nutmeg, baking powder, and salt. Set aside.

In large bowl, beat butter with ¾ cup sugar until light. Beat in egg and vanilla. Stir in dry ingredients, mixing to blend thoroughly.

In small bowl, combine remaining 2 tablespoons sugar and cinnamon. Pinch off pieces of dough and roll between palms of hands into 1-inch balls. Roll each ball in sugar mixture and place on prepared baking sheets. Bake about 15 minutes or until golden. Cool on baking sheet 1 minute. Transfer to wire racks to cool.

MAKES ABOUT 36

KIDS'
COOKIES

COCONUT CHERRY HAYSTACKS

Sticky, gooey, chewy golden stacks of coconut—what could be better?

1 cup walnuts, toasted and roughly chopped
2½ cups shredded sweetened coconut
½ cup dried sour cherries
½ cup semisweet chocolate chips
7 ounces sweetened condensed milk

Preheat oven to 325 degrees F. Line cookie sheets with parchment paper or use nonstick pan.

In mixing bowl combine nuts, coconut, dried cherries and chocolate chips. Pour in condensed milk and stir well to combine.

Drop generous tablespoonfuls of batter on cookie sheet and flatten lightly with back of spoon. Bake 15 to 20 minutes, until coconut is pale golden and bottoms are light brown. Transfer to racks to cool.

MAKES 20

Baking Times

Since cookies are so small, baking time is crucial. Two minutes can mean the difference between delightfully crisp and hopelessly burnt.

Though all our recipes are tested, there is still no accounting for equipment and oven differences. Always begin checking a few minutes before the recommended baking time has elapsed. In general, darker cookie sheets and those with sides will cause cookies to cook faster, and if you are using more than one shelf in the oven, the cookies on the top one will brown faster. Double shelving totally throws things off so keep a careful watch. As for pans, we are partial to the light, double-sheeted "cushionaires."

DOUBLE CHOCOLATE WALNUT DROPS

For children (and adults) who like their chocolate deep, dark, mysterious and delicious and their cookie making as easy as pie. Here is a good, hand-stirred batter.

3 ounces unsweetened chocolate, in chunks
1 stick butter
1½ cups sugar
2 eggs
1 teaspoon vanilla
1 cup all-purpose flour
½ cup plus 2 tablespoons Dutch process cocoa (see p. 53)
½ teaspoon baking soda
¾ cup walnuts, roughly chopped
½ cup semisweet chocolate chips

Preheat oven to 375 degrees F. Grease
cookie sheets.

In heavy, medium saucepan, melt chocolate
and butter over low heat, stirring frequently.
Let cool 5 minutes and pour into large
mixing bowl.

Whisk in sugar until blended, then eggs, one
at a time. Stir in remaining ingredients, one at
a time, with a wooden spoon. The batter will
be quite stiff.

Drop by generous teaspoonfuls on prepared
sheets. Bake 10 to 12 minutes, just until edges
set. Transfer to racks to cool.

MAKES 36

GRANDMA EDLUND'S GINGERSNAPS

Thanks to Julia Davis's grandma for a cookie with just enough spice, crackle, and snap.

3/4 cup vegetable shortening
1 cup brown sugar
1/4 cup molasses
1 egg
2 cups all-purpose flour
1/2 teaspoon salt
2 teaspoons baking soda
1 tablespoon ground ginger
1 teaspoon cinnamon
1/4 teaspoon ground cloves
granulated sugar for rolling

Preheat oven to 350 degrees F. Lightly grease cookie sheets.

Cream together shortening and brown sugar. Beat in molasses and egg.

In another bowl, combine flour, salt, baking soda, cinnamon, ginger, and cloves. Add to creamed mixture and slowly beat until well combined.

Break dough into 1½ teaspoon-sized pieces and roll between palms to make small balls. Roll each in sugar to coat and place on prepared cookie sheets, leaving space for spreading. Bake 10 to 12 minutes, until cookies are flat, light brown and cracked on top. For a crisper snap, bake until dark brown. Transfer to racks to cool.

MAKES ABOUT 40

LEMON ICE BOX COOKIES

For those who believe their lemon wafers can never be too thin, too crisp or too lemony. The frosting is optional but delicious.

1 stick butter, softened
⅔ cup sugar
1 egg yolk
1 tablespoon grated lemon zest
1½ teaspoons grated lime zest
1 teaspoon vanilla
½ cup all-purpose flour
½ cup plus 2 tablespoons cake flour
¼ teaspoon salt

FROSTING

¾ cup confectioners' sugar
1 tablespoon plus 1 teaspoon
    lemon juice

Cream together butter and sugar until light and fluffy. Beat in egg yolk, two zests, and vanilla.

In another bowl,
combine two flours and salt.
Add to butter mixture and slowly
beat until flour disappears and
dough holds together. Remove, press
into ball and divide in two. Handling lightly,
on floured board, press each piece into small log,
about $1\frac{1}{2}$ x 4-inches. Wrap each in plastic and
chill 1 hour or as long as a week.

To bake, preheat oven to 375 degrees F. Lightly
grease 2 cookie sheets and line with parchment
paper, if desired. Cut each log across width into
$\frac{3}{8}$-inch slices. Arrange slices on cookie sheet, 1 inch
apart, and bake about 10 minutes, until edges are just
golden and centers set. Transfer to racks to cool.

For frosting: In small bowl whisk together sugar
and lemon juice until smooth and thick enough to
spread. (Thin with a few drops of lemon juice or
thicken with more sugar as necessary.)

Hold each cooled cookie along the edges and
spread a thin layer of frosting with small
spatula or butter knife. Dry and store in tins.
MAKES 30

OATMEAL TOFFEE THINS

Look for hard candy toffee bits in the baking section of the supermarket.

1 stick butter, softened
½ cup sugar
½ cup brown sugar
1 egg
1 cup all-purpose flour
¾ cup rolled oats
½ teaspoon baking soda
½ teaspoon salt
1 cup toffee bits
1 cup semisweet chocolate chips
½ cup chopped walnuts

Preheat oven to 350 degrees F. Lightly grease cookie sheets.

Cream together butter
and two sugars until light and
fluffy. Beat in egg.

In another bowl, combine flour,
oats, baking soda, and salt. Add to butter
mixture and mix until combined. Stir in toffee,
followed by chips and nuts. Drop by tablespoonfuls
on sheets, leaving space. Bake 13 to 15 minutes,
until golden brown on edges. Let cool on sheets
2 minutes to set and then transfer to racks.

MAKES 40

Greasing the Sheets

*For the sake of convenience we use cooking spray
rather than butter or shortening to coat cookie sheets.
All are okay.*

*Greasing or coating the sheet increases cookie spread
and makes it easier to remove sticky cookies. Very rich
cookies, such as shortbreads or puff pastries, are baked on
uncoated pans to minimize spread. Parchment paper,
available in rolls at the supermarket, is great for
faultless cookie and brownie removal. We like to
lightly coat the sheet first to make the paper stick.*

CANDY JUMBLES

This version of the classic oatmeal raisin cookie is enhanced by every preschooler's favorite vice—chocolate candy.

1 stick butter, softened
½ cup brown sugar
1 egg
½ teaspoon vanilla
1 cup all purpose flour
½ cup rolled oats
½ teaspoon baking soda
½ teaspoon salt
1 cup candy-coated
  chocolate bits
1 cup raisins
½ cup chopped walnuts

Preheat oven to 350 degrees F.

Lightly grease cookie sheets.

Cream together butter and sugar until smooth. Beat in egg and vanilla.

In another bowl, combine flour, oats, baking soda and salt. Add to butter mixture and mix until thoroughly combined. Lightly stir in chocolate pieces, raisins, and nuts.

Drop scant tablespoonfuls onto prepared sheets, 2 inches apart. Bake 12 to 14 minutes, until edges are golden brown. Cool on racks.

MAKES 36

S'MORE BARS

Here is a bake-ahead version of every camper's favorite marshmallow sandwich.

1 stick butter
¼ cup brown sugar
1 teaspoon vanilla
2 cups graham cracker crumbs
2 cups miniature marshmallows
4 (1.55-ounce) milk chocolate
candy bars

Preheat oven to 250 degrees F. Line 8-inch square baking pan with buttered foil.

In medium saucepan, combine butter and brown sugar. Cook over medium heat until sugar dissolves and mixture is bubbly. Stir in vanilla, cracker crumbs, and marshmallows.

Cook and stir just until
marshmallows begin to melt.
Spread evenly in prepared pan.
With back of large spoon, press mixture
to make even layer. Set candy bars, side by
side, in single layer to cover top. Place in oven
5 minutes or until chocolate is shiny all over.
With spatula, spread chocolate to evenly cover top.
Remove and chill in refrigerator. Cut into bars.

MAKES 16

On Fats

*We prefer butter for its wholesome flavor and
spreading ability in cookies. Margarine can always be
substituted but use the solid, not whipped, variety and
adjust salt accordingly. Since these recipes were tested
with unsalted butter, omit salt in the recipe if using
salted butter or margarine.*

*Where vegetable shortening is called for, it is being
used for the crumbly, crunchy texture it adds to
cookies. It does not add flavor.*

CRISPY RICE BARS

We consider these one of the great culinary contributions of the 1950s!

3 cups miniature marshmallows
½ stick butter
1 teaspoon vanilla
6 cups toasted rice cereal
½ cup currants

Line 13 x 9-inch baking pan with buttered wax paper or foil.

In large saucepan, combine marshmallows and butter. Set over low heat, stirring constantly, until marshmallows are melted. Remove from heat and stir in vanilla. Gently stir in 3 cups cereal until evenly distributed. Stir in remaining cereal and currants. Turn into prepared pan. With back of large spoon press mixture into pan to create even layer.

Cool. Lift from pan and cut into bars.

MAKES 24

COOKIE CLAY

This uncooked dough can be molded, pressed, played with, and eaten. It's a perfect rainy afternoon's entertainment for any toddler.

1 cup quick-cooking oats
1 cup peanut butter
1½ cups non-fat dry milk powder
½ cup honey
1 teaspoon vanilla
½ teaspoon cinnamon
nuts, small candies, raisins and coconut
    for decorating

In large bowl stir oats, peanut butter, milk powder, honey, vanilla, and cinnamon to blend thoroughly.

Hand mold into dinosaurs, coiled snakes, teddy bears, or other creatures. Decorate as desired. Store unused portion in refrigerator.

MAKES 2½ CUPS

ROLL'N'CUT COOKIES

Here is a fairly easy dough for rolling and cutting holiday cookies.

> 3 cups all-purpose flour
> 2 teaspoons cream of tartar
> 1 teaspoon baking soda
> 2 sticks butter, softened
> 2 eggs
> 1 cup sugar
> 1 teaspoon vanilla
> Colored frosting, sugars, and
>   decorative candies

Preheat oven to 350 degrees F. Grease and flour baking sheets.

Sift flour, cream of tartar and baking soda into large bowl. Add butter, using 2 knives or pastry blender, until mixture is like coarse crumbs.

In separate bowl, beat eggs, sugar, and vanilla to blend. Stir egg mixture into flour mixture, blending well. Divide dough into thirds. Wrap each piece in plastic and chill 10 to 15 minutes.

On lightly floured surface, roll out dough, one at a time, to $\frac{1}{8}$-inch thickness. Cut with floured cookie cutters. Place cookies, 2 inches apart, on prepared baking sheets and bake 10 minutes or until golden. Transfer to wire racks and cool completely. Decorate as desired.

MAKES ABOUT 36 THREE-INCH COOKIES

CHOCOLATE PIZZA

The perfect ending to a pizza party. Make sure the kids help spread the dough and sprinkle their favorite toppings.

4 (1-ounce) squares unsweetened chocolate, coarsely chopped
1 (1-ounce) square semisweet chocolate, coarsely chopped
¾ cup vegetable shortening
1 cup sugar
½ cup milk
¾ cup all-purpose flour
½ teaspoon salt
3 eggs
⅓ cup shredded, sweetened coconut
¼ cup semisweet chocolate chips
¼ cup vanilla chips
¼ cup coarsely chopped pecans

Preheat oven to 325 F. Grease 11-inch pizza pan.

In saucepan, combine chopped chocolates and shortening.

Place over low heat until melted. Stir in ½ cup sugar and milk, mixing to blend well. Cool to lukewarm.

Combine flour and salt. Set aside.

In large bowl, beat eggs until lemon colored. Beat in remaining ½ cup sugar. Beat in cooled chocolate mixture until blended. Stir in flour mixture. Turn out onto prepared pan, spreading to make even layer to within ½ inch of rim.

Combine coconut, candy pieces and pecans. Sprinkle evenly over dough. Bake 25 minutes. Cool, then cut into wedges.

MAKES 16

BROWNIES
AND BARS

MONKEY BARS

Here is an easy way to please the after-school crowd.

½ stick butter, softened
½ cup brown sugar
1 egg
¾ cup mashed ripe bananas (about 2)
1¼ cups all-purpose flour
4 ounces semisweet chocolate,
    coarsely chopped
⅓ cup shredded sweetened coconut
    (optional)

Preheat oven to 350 degrees F. Grease 9-inch square baking pan.

Beat butter and sugar until fluffy. Beat in egg, then bananas. Gradually beat in flour. Stir in chocolate.

Spread batter evenly in prepared pan. Bake about 25 minutes or until toothpick inserted near center comes out clean.

Cool in pan and cut into
bars. If using coconut, sprinkle
over top during last 10 minutes of
baking. Lift from pan and cut into bars.

MAKES 16

Chocolate Baking Tips

Since chocolate has a tendency to scare new cooks,
here are a few pointers. Chocolate can be melted in an
ordinary heavy, bottomed pan—no double boiler necessary—if butter is melted along with it. Always melt
chocolate over low heat, stirring frequently, to keep the
temperature down.

Compared to chocolate, cocoa produces lighter flavor
and color in baked goods. Dutch process cocoa,available
in the baking section of the supermarket, is best for
baking since it gives a darker color and better flavor
than the others. Bear in mind that all cocoa is
unsweetened.

LEMON BARS

The classic, no equipment, one bowl, lemon lover's dream bar.

CRUST
1 cup all-purpose flour
¼ cup confectioners' sugar
1 stick butter, softened
½ teaspoon grated lemon zest

TOPPING
3 eggs
1 cup sugar
½ cup lemon juice
1 tablespoon grated lemon zest
2 tablespoons all-purpose flour
½ teaspoon baking powder
confectioners' sugar for dusting

Preheat oven to 350 degrees F.

Combine flour and sugar in mixing bowl. Cut butter into tablespoon-sized pieces and add to flour, along with zest. Combine with fingers or pastry blender until dough is formed. Press evenly into ungreased 8-inch square baking pan. Bake 18 minutes, until edges are golden and sides start to pull away from pan. Cool on rack 5 minutes. Reduce oven to 325 degrees F.

Lightly whisk eggs in bowl. Whisk in sugar, followed by lemon juice and zest. Stir in flour and baking powder. Pour over baked crust and return to oven. Bake 25 minutes, until top is set when pressed in center. Let cool on rack, dust with confectioners' sugar and cut into squares to serve. Store in refrigerator.

MAKES 20

FUDGE MINT BROWNIES

A thin layer of glossy mint chocolate frosting elevates these fudgy brownies to the upper echelon of browniedom.

6 ounces semisweet chocolate, chopped
3 tablespoons butter
¾ cup sugar
3½ tablespoons water
2 eggs
¾ cup all-purpose flour
¾ teaspoon salt
1 cup white chocolate chips

GLAZE
4 ounces semisweet chocolate, chopped
2 tablespoons butter
2 tablespoons water
½ teaspoon mint extract
¼ teaspoon vanilla

Preheat oven to 325 degrees F. Grease an 8-inch square baking pan and line with parchment paper.

In heavy, medium saucepan, combine chocolate, butter, sugar and water. Cook over low heat, stirring frequently, until melted and smooth. Let cool and then pour into large mixing bowl.

Whisk eggs into chocolate mixture. Stir in flour and salt. Then stir in chips. Pour into lined pan and smooth into even layer. Bake 30 minutes, until sides begin to pull away and center is set. Cool in pan on rack for 1 hour.

To make glaze, melt chocolate, butter and water together in small heavy saucepan over low flame, stirring frequently. Stir in extracts and remove from heat. Let sit while brownies cool. When cool, invert brownies on rack, peel paper and turn over onto serving plate. Spread thin layer of glaze over top. Refrigerate until set and shiny, about 30 minutes, then cut into small squares.

MAKES 25

BUTTERSCOTCH BLONDIES

Here is the classic caramel and vanilla-flavored brownie for non-chocolate people.

1 ¼ cups all-purpose flour
½ teaspoon baking soda
½ teaspoon salt
½ stick butter, softened
½ cup sugar
½ cup brown sugar
1 egg
½ teaspoon vanilla
1 cup butterscotch pieces

Preheat oven to 350 degrees F. Grease 9-inch square baking pan.

Sift together flour, baking soda, and salt. Set aside.

In bowl of mixer, beat butter and sugars until fluffy.

Add egg and vanilla and beat well. Gradually add dry ingredients, beating on low speed until thoroughly blended.

Spread batter in prepared baking pan. Sprinkle butterscotch pieces evenly over top. Bake 5 minutes or just until candy pieces are shiny and soft. With knife, swirl pieces into batter to create marbled effect. Return to oven and bake 15 to 20 minutes longer. Cool then cut into bars.

MAKES 16

BASIC BROWNIES

*Leave it to American ingenuity to invent the
one-bowl, no-special-equipment miracle of
chocolate and nuts called the brownie—our
favorite accompaniment to milk.*

4 ounces unsweetened chocolate,
   broken up
1½ sticks butter
4 eggs
2 cups sugar
¾ teaspoon vanilla
1 cup all-purpose flour
½ teaspoon salt
1 to 2 cups chopped walnuts

Preheat oven to 350 degrees F. Grease
and flour 9 x 12-inch baking pan and line
with parchment.

In medium heavy saucepan, melt chocolate and butter over low heat, stirring frequently. Set aside to cool.

In large bowl, whisk eggs until smooth. Whisk in sugar and then vanilla. Pour in cooled chocolate mixture and whisk to blend. Add flour and salt. Stir to combine and then stir in nuts.

Pour into prepared pan and bake 25 to 30 minutes, until toothpick inserted in center comes out with moist particles clinging to it. (Be careful not to overbake.)

Cool pan on rack 1 hour. Cut into bars and remove. Dust with confectioners' sugar, if desired.

MAKES ABOUT 20

LINZER BARS

This luxurious, nutty crust topped with red raspberry jam is an adaptation of the classic Viennese coffeehouse tart.

1 stick butter, softened
½ cup sugar
1 egg yolk
1 tablespoon grated orange zest
½ teaspoon almond extract
1 ¼ cups all-purpose flour
½ cup ground almonds
½ teaspoon baking powder
1 teaspoon cinnamon
¼ teaspoon salt
¾ cup raspberry jam

TOPPING

¼ cup all-purpose flour
¼ cup ground almonds
2 tablespoons brown sugar
3 tablespoons butter, softened

Preheat oven to 350 degrees F.

To make crust, cream together butter and sugar. Beat in egg yolk, orange zest, and almond extract.

In another bowl, combine flour, ground almonds, baking powder, cinnamon, and salt. Stir and toss with fork. Add to creamed mixture and slowly beat until crumbly dough is formed. Press dough into ungreased, 8-inch square cake pan, building up edges a bit to prevent spills. Spread raspberry jam over crust.

In another small bowl, make topping. Toss together flour, ground almonds and brown sugar. Then cut butter into 6 pieces and mix with fingertips or pastry blender to make a crumbly topping. Sprinkle over jam layer and bake 40 minutes. Cool in pan on rack. Cut into squares and carefully remove with spatula. Wrap in foil to store.

MAKES 16

APRICOT COCONUT BARS

We love the combination of tart, chewy, and sweet in these rich bar cookies.

FILLING
1½ cups dried apricots, coarsely chopped
1 cup water
¼ cup sugar
3 tablespoons lemon juice

CRUST
1½ cups all-purpose flour
¼ cup brown sugar
¼ cup unsweetened, shredded coconut
¼ teaspoon salt
9 tablespoons cold butter

TOPPING
½ cup unsweetened, shredded coconut
⅓ cup semisweet mini morsels

Combine apricots and water in medium saucepan. Bring to boil and cook about 5 minutes until water is absorbed. Stir in sugar and lemon juice, cook 2 minutes longer and remove from heat. Let cool.

Preheat oven to 350 degrees F.

In mixing bowl, combine flour, brown sugar, coconut and salt. Cut butter into ¼-inch slices and blend into flour mixture with fingertips or pastry blender until crumbly dough is formed. Press into 8-inch square, ungreased pan, building up the sides slightly to form an edge. Bake crust 15 minutes. Remove from oven, leaving oven on.

Spread apricot mixture evenly over crust. Mix together coconut and chocolate chips in small bowl and sprinkle on top. Return to oven and bake 15 minutes, until coconut is golden brown. Let cool in pan on rack. Cut into squares and carefully remove with spatula.

MAKES 25

OATMEAL BERRY BARS

These easy-to-mix granola-type bars are ideal for packing in lunch boxes or picnic baskets.

1½ cups rolled oats
1 cup all-purpose flour
¾ cup brown sugar
½ teaspoon baking soda
½ teaspoon salt
1 stick plus 6 tablespoons butter, melted
1 cup dried cranberries
1 tablespoon grated orange zest
½ cup semisweet chocolate chips

Preheat oven to 350 degrees F. Line a 9-inch square baking pan with parchment paper.

In large bowl, combine oats, flour, sugar, baking soda, and salt. Pour in butter and stir well to evenly moisten. Stir in cranberries, orange zest, and chips. Press into prepared baking pan, and bake 40 minutes until edges begin to brown. Cool 1 hour. Cut into squares and remove.

MAKES 24

CHOCOLATE FRUIT CRISPIES

*Does anyone ever outgrow their need
for icky, sticky, marshmallow bar cookies?
We don't think so.*

> 6 cups toasted rice cereal
> ½ cup raisins
> ½ cup finely chopped, dried apricots
> 1 (10-ounce) bag large marshmallows
> ½ cup semisweet chocolate chips
> 2 tablespoons milk

In large bowl, combine cereal, raisins, and apricots.

In medium saucepan, combine marshmallows, chocolate chips, and milk. Cook over low heat, stirring frequently, until melted.

Pour hot chocolate mixture over cereal mixture and thoroughly mix. Spread evenly in greased 12 x 8-inch pan. Cover and chill until set. Cut into 2-inch squares.

MAKES 24

INTERNATIONAL

GINGER HAZELNUT BISCOTTI

Here is a rich biscotti—chock full of nuts and spice.

1 cup hazelnuts
1 stick butter, softened
⅓ cup brown sugar
2 eggs
1 teaspoon almond extract
2½ cups all-purpose flour
1½ teaspoons baking powder
1 tablespoon ground ginger
1½ teaspoons cinnamon
½ teaspoon salt
1 egg white
2 tablespoons sugar mixed with
    ¼ teaspoon cinnamon

Preheat oven to 350 degrees F.
Spread hazelnuts on baking tray and bake
10 to 15 minutes, until skins start to blister.

Let cool, then place in sieve and rub against screen to remove skins. Finely grind half the nuts and roughly chop other half.

In bowl of electric mixer, cream butter and sugar until light. Beat in eggs, one at a time, and almond extract.

In another bowl, combine finely ground hazelnuts, flour, baking powder, ginger, cinnamon, and salt. Add to creamed mixture and slowly beat until dough is formed. Beat in chopped hazelnuts.

On lightly floured board, knead dough into ball and cut in half. Press each piece into 10 x 4-inch loaf and transfer to uncoated baking sheet. Whisk egg white until foamy and brush on loaf tops. Sprinkle with cinnamon sugar.

Bake about 35 minutes, until tops are golden and loaves firm. Cool on sheet about 10 minutes. Transfer loaves to cutting board and with chef's knife, cut into ½-inch slices across width.

Place cookies on sheet, cut side up, and bake 10 minutes longer on each side, until golden.
MAKES 24

MARGE'S MANDELBROT

The Jewish answer to biscotti, a just-dry-enough loaf cookie, packed with chocolate chips and a hint of vanilla to round out the flavors. Thanks to Marge Schneider, of Deerfield Beach, Florida.

½ cup vegetable oil
½ cup sugar
2 eggs
1 teaspoon vanilla
1 cup chocolate chips
2 cups all-purpose flour
2 teaspoons baking powder
¼ cup finely chopped walnuts
¼ teaspoon salt

Preheat oven to 350 degrees F. Lightly grease large cookie sheet.

In large bowl, whisk together oil and sugar. Whisk in eggs, vanilla, and chocolate chips. Set aside.

In another bowl, combine flour, baking powder, walnuts and salt. Add flour mixture to liquid mixture and stir until evenly combined and flour disappears.

Gently knead on well-floured board and divide dough into four pieces. Shape each into a small loaf, about 3 x 5 inches. Transfer to prepared baking sheet and bake until set and slightly golden along edges, 40 to 45 minutes. Remove, leaving oven on, and let cool on sheet 10 minutes.

Transfer loaves to cutting board and cut with sharp knife across width into ½-inch slices. Return cookies to baking sheet, cut side up and bake an additional 5 minutes on each side. Let cool and store in tins.

MAKES 36

IDA'S RUGELACH

These traditional miniature pastries filled with jelly, cinnamon and nuts are easier to roll than most. They come from Helene's mom— one of the world's great rugelach makers.

PASTRY
2 sticks butter, softened
1 cup sour cream
2¼ cups all-purpose flour

FILLING
1 cup walnuts, finely chopped
½ cup raisins, chopped
¼ cup sugar
½ teaspoon cinnamon
1 cup apricot preserves
1 egg white
¼ cup sugar mixed with ½ teaspoon
  cinnamon for sprinkling

Cream together
butter and sour cream
until light and creamy.
Slowly beat in flour until
dough is smooth and elastic. Lightly
knead on floured board; form disk,
cover with plastic wrap and chill at least 1 hour.

In medium bowl, combine nuts, raisins, sugar,
and cinnamon.

When ready to bake, cut dough into 4 equal
parts. Chill three. On lightly floured board, roll each
into 5 x 12-inch loaves. Coat center of strip, lengthwise, with about ¼ cup apricot preserves. Sprinkle
preserves with raisin nut mixture. Fold over one side,
lengthwise, and then the other to enclose filling.
Lightly press edges and ends to seal. Brush top with
egg white and sprinkle with cinnamon-sugar mixture.

Cut across width into 1-inch slices and carefully
transfer pieces to uncoated cookie sheet. Chill ½ hour.

Preheat oven to 400 degrees F. Bake, 1 sheet at a
time, 10 minutes. Reduce temperature to 375 F and
bake 15 to 20 minutes longer, until golden.
Transfer to racks to cool.
MAKES 40

CHINESE ALMOND COOKIES

These look just like the cookies served in Chinese restaurants—they taste even better!

1½ cups all-purpose flour
½ teaspoon baking soda
½ teaspoon salt
½ cup vegetable shortening
½ cup sugar
1 egg
½ teaspoon almond extract
12 almonds, blanched and separated into halves
1 egg yolk combined with 2 teaspoons water

Preheat oven to 375 degrees F.
Sift together flour, soda, and salt. Set aside.
Cream shortening with sugar until light.
Add egg and almond extract and beat to blend.
Stir in dry ingredients and mix thoroughly.

Pinch off pieces of dough
and roll between palms of hands
to make 1-inch balls. Place on
ungreased baking sheets and flatten
with palm of hand. Place an almond
half in center of each cookie. Brush tops
with yolk mixture.

Bake 15 minutes or until golden. Transfer
to racks to cool.

MAKES ABOUT 24

On Sweeteners

Granulated white sugar is the basic sugar for cookie baking. Brown sugar, which is white sugar soaked in molasses, can be substituted for white, but it will change the results slightly. It adds caramel color and flavor, and a slight chewiness. For tender, crisper cookies use all white sugar.

Liquid sweeteners like molasses, honey, and maple syrup should not be substituted for sugar since they totally change the proportion of liquid to dry ingredients—which can mean messy meltdowns on the oven floor.

MEXICAN WEDDING CAKES

These puffs of powdered sugar are a traditional Christmas cookie.

1 stick butter, softened
3 tablespoons confectioners' sugar
1½ teaspoons vanilla
⅛ teaspoon salt
1 cup all-purpose flour
½ cup finely chopped toasted hazelnuts
confectioners' sugar for dipping

Preheat oven to 350 degrees F. Grease baking sheets.

Cream butter with sugar. Stir in vanilla, salt, flour, and nuts. Dough will be stiff. Pinch off pieces of dough and roll between palms of hands to make 1-inch balls. Place on prepared baking sheets and bake

10 to 12 minutes or until light golden. While still warm, roll cookies in additional powdered sugar.

MAKES ABOUT 30

On Flours

   Unbleached all-purpose flour is our basic cookie-making flour. Here are the characteristics some other flours and grains can bring to cookie-making experiments:

   Cake flour adds a soft, light, melt-in-your-mouth texture as does a few spoonfuls of cornstarch; cornmeal adds grittiness, the color yellow and a hint of sweetness; whole wheat flour adds bulk, brown color, and nutty flavor; and oats add chewiness.

FLORENTINES

These elegant chocolate-coated wafers are special enough to serve as a light dessert.

⅓ cup heavy cream
¼ stick butter
3 tablespoons sugar
½ cup finely chopped blanched almonds
¼ cup finely chopped candied orange peel
¼ cup all-purpose flour
4 ounces semisweet chocolate, melted

Preheat oven to 350 degrees F. Grease and flour baking sheets.

In saucepan, combine cream, butter, and sugar. Stir over medium heat until sugar dissolves and butter is melted.

Remove from heat and stir in almonds, orange peel, and flour.

Drop rounded teaspoonfuls of batter about 3 inches apart onto prepared baking sheets. Bake 8 to 10 minutes or until golden, watching carefully to prevent burning. Carefully transfer to wire racks to cool completely.

With spatula, spread chocolate over bottom of each cookie. Cool chocolate side up, on rack until hardened. Store in an airtight container with wax paper between layers.

MAKES ABOUT 24

On Leaveners

Many cookies contain no leavening. Most contain very little. In general, baking soda produces thin, crisp cookies; baking powder produces the puffy, cakey variety.

CAT'S TONGUES

Leave it to the French to come up with such a delicately textured and poetically named cookie. If you don't have a pastry bag, you can substitute a ziplock bag with a 1/4-inch slit cut at one corner.

6 tablespoons all-purpose flour
1/4 teaspoon salt
1/2 stick butter, softened
6 tablespoons sugar
1/2 teaspoon vanilla
1/4 teaspoon almond extract
3 egg whites
1/2 cup finely chopped or ground
blanched almonds

Preheat oven to 425 degrees F. Grease and flour baking sheets.

Sift flour with salt. Set aside.

Beat butter and sugar until fluffy. Beat in vanilla and almond extract. Set aside.

In another bowl, beat egg whites until soft peaks form.

Alternately stir 2 tablespoons flour mixture and half of egg whites into butter mixture, stirring well after each addition. Stir in almonds. Spoon mixture into pastry bag fitted with ¼-inch plain tube and pipe batter in 3-inch lengths onto prepared baking sheets. Bake about 6 minutes or until edges are golden. Cool on racks.

MAKES ABOUT 36

PALMIERS

*Puff pastry elephant ears from France are
best served the same day they are baked for
maximum flakiness.*

1 (17¼-ounce) package frozen
   puff pastry
1 cup sugar

Thaw frozen pastry according to
package directions.

Sprinkle work surface with ⅛-inch
thick layer of sugar.

Place one sheet pastry on sugar and
sprinkle top with more sugar. Run rolling
pin lightly over dough to help sugar
adhere. Fold in each long side of dough so
edges meet in center. Sprinkle with sugar.
Fold one half over the other, as if closing

a book. Press layers together with palms of hands. Wrap in plastic and chill until firm.

Preheat oven to 400 F. Line baking sheets with parchment paper or use nonstick pans.

With sharp knife, cut dough into ¼-inch thick slices. Press cut edges into sugar. Place on prepared baking sheets. Bake about 12 minutes or until golden. Immediately transfer to rack to cool.

MAKES ABOUT 48

RICE MADELEINES

This traditional French cookie is one of our favorite late afternoon treats.

1 cup whole blanched almonds, lightly toasted
¾ cup sweetened flaked coconut
1½ cups sugar
3 cups cooked rice, chilled
3 egg whites

Preheat oven to 350 degrees F. Coat madeleine pans or miniature muffin tins with cooking spray.

In food processor, chop almonds until ground. Add coconut and sugar and process until finely minced. Add rice; pulse to blend. Add egg whites; pulse to blend. Spoon mixture into pans, filling to top. Bake 25 to 30 minutes or until lightly browned. Cool completely in pans on wire rack. Run sharp knife around each madeleine and remove from pan.

MAKES 36

Cookies by Category

Drop cookies, such as the classic chocolate chip, have thick, rich batters and are literally dropped from a spoon onto the cookie sheet for baking.

Rolled cookies, like Christmas sugar cookies and gingerbread people, are a bit more demanding since the dough has to be rolled and then cut. A few tips for rolling: cold pastry is easier to roll; lightly dust board and rolling pin with flour to prevent sticking; place a sheet of plastic wrap over dough to prevent sticking; always handle lightly and keep re-rolling to a minimum since dough gets tougher with handling.

Refrigerator cookies are similar to rolled cookies but easier to handle since the rich dough is first shaped into a log, then chilled and sliced for baking. The results are thin, crisp wafers or thick chewy rounds depending on the thickness of the slice. Great for last-minute cookie baking.

Bar cookies are the fastest since the batter is poured or patted into a pan and then baked and cut into bars. Brownies are the classic bar cookie.

GROWN-UP
TASTES

SESAME LOGS

This traditional Sicilian sesame seed cookie, known as a regina, makes a nice light breakfast treat.

¼ cup vegetable shortening
½ cup sugar
1 egg yolk
¾ teaspoon vanilla
¼ teaspoon almond extract
¼ cup milk
¾ cup all-purpose flour
1 cup cake flour
¼ teaspoon baking powder
2 egg whites
½ cup sesame seeds

Preheat oven to 350 degrees F. Grease cookie sheet.

Beat together shortening and sugar until light and fluffy. Add egg yolk, vanilla and almond extracts and beat. Mix in milk.

In another bowl, combine flours and baking powder. Add to liquid mixture and beat until smooth.

Turn onto floured board and knead lightly to form a smooth disk. Divide into 12 pieces and roll each between palms to form 3½-inch long cylinders.

In small bowl, lightly whisk egg whites until frothy. Place sesame seeds in small, wide bowl. Dip each cylinder first in egg whites, and then in sesame seeds to coat all over. Lay on baking sheet, 1-inch apart. Bake about 20 minutes, until set but not brown. Cool on racks.

MAKES 16

CORNMEAL ANISEED CRESCENTS

These cakey yellow cookies have a subtle hint of anise.

1 ½ sticks butter, softened
¾ cup sugar
2 eggs
2 teaspoons grated lemon zest
2 cups cake flour
½ cup plus 2 tablespoons cornmeal
½ teaspoon baking powder
½ teaspoon salt
2 tablespoons aniseeds

Beat together butter and sugar until light and fluffy. Beat in eggs, one at a time.

In another bowl, combine flour, cornmeal, salt and aniseed. Add to butter mixture and beat well. Chill 1 hour.

Preheat oven to 325 degrees F. Grease cookie sheets.

Break dough into walnut-sized chunks. Roll each between palms to form cylinder, place on sheet and then bend to form crescent. Bake 15 minutes, until set but not brown. Transfer to racks to cool.

MAKES 36

PUMPKIN SPICE COOKIES

These moist little cakes are exceptionally delicate-tasting for a pumpkin pastry. Don't be put off by the length of the ingredient list. They are very easy to make.

1 stick butter, softened
¾ cup brown sugar
1 egg
1 teaspoon vanilla
1 cup canned, pumpkin puree
2 cups all-purpose flour
1 teaspoon baking powder
½ teaspoon baking soda
½ teaspoon salt
1 teaspoon cinnamon
½ teaspoon nutmeg
½ teaspoon ground ginger
¼ teaspoon ground clove
1 cup raisins
1 cup chopped walnuts

Preheat oven to 350 degrees F.
Lightly grease cookie sheets.

Cream together butter and brown sugar until smooth. Beat in egg and vanilla. Beat in pumpkin puree.

In another bowl, combine flour, baking powder, baking soda, salt, cinnamon, nutmeg, ginger, and clove. Add to butter mixture and beat well to combine. Add raisins and nuts in 2 batches, mixing between additions.

Drop by tablespoonfuls onto prepared sheets. Bake about 18 minutes, until set, not browned. Transfer to racks to cool.

MAKES 32

CINNAMON PASTRY CRESCENTS

These quick pastries are great when unexpected guests drop in.

1 (15-ounce) box refrigerated, pre-rolled pie crusts
½ stick butter, softened
4 tablespoons sugar
2 tablespoons cinnamon

Preheat oven to 400 degrees F.

Lay two crusts on lightly floured surface and spread each with half of butter. Sprinkle with sugar then cinnamon.

Cut each crust into 16 wedges. Starting at wide end, roll each wedge, bending ends down slightly to create crescent shape. Arrange on uncoated baking sheet and bake about 15 minutes or until golden. Transfer to racks to cool.

MAKES 32